Scholastic

Clifford THE BIG RED DOG®

Share-and-Be-Fair

STICKER BOOK

Adapted by Kimberly Weinberger
Illustrated by John Kurtz

**Based on the Scholastic book series
"Clifford The Big Red Dog"
by Norman Bridwell**

From the television script "Clifford's Credos"
by Sindy McKay Swerdlove

SCHOLASTIC INC.
Cartwheel B·O·O·K·S®

New York   Toronto   London   Auckland   Sydney   Mexico City
New Delhi   Hong Kong

ISBN 0-439-22944-8

Library of Congress Cataloging-in-Publication Data available

10 9 8 7 6 5 4 3 2 1   01 02 03 04 05

Printed in the U.S.A.
First printing, February 2001

2

Hi! My name is Emily Elizabeth.
That's my dog, Clifford, and those are
his friends Cleo and T-Bone.
They have lots of great times
playing together.
Let's go join the fun!

*Find a sticker of a picnic basket and
put it on this page.*

3

Playing a game with friends can mean working as a team. I remember the day Cleo learned about **COOPERATION** during a soccer game at the park. . . .

Find stickers of soccer goals and place them at both ends of the field.

4

Cleo had the ball.
But Manny was blocking her path
to the goal.
"Kick it to me, Cleo!" T-Bone called.

*Can you find a sticker of T-Bone
and put it on this page?*

Cleo did not want to pass
the ball to T-Bone.
I can score by myself! she thought.
But when she tried to make the goal,
Manny blocked it.

Find a sticker of the soccer ball and place it in Manny's hands.

6

During a time-out, Clifford said, "Cleo, maybe next time you should pass the ball to T-Bone. We'll do better if we work together as a team."

Can you find stickers of clouds and butterflies and put them on this page?

Cleo knew that Clifford was right. "I'm sorry," she said. "Next time I'll be sure to do what's best for all of us."

Find a sticker of Cleo and place it next to Clifford.

Later, Cleo got the ball again.
Seeing Rex blocking her way to the goal,
she quickly passed the ball to T-Bone.
And T-Bone scored!

*Help T-Bone score by placing a sticker of him on the field
and putting a sticker of the ball in the goal.*

9

Clifford, Cleo, and T-Bone
all had great fun that day.
Once they knew the importance
of **COOPERATION**, they were
a winning team!

PARK

Can you find a sticker of the setting sun and place it in the sky?

Playing fairly makes playing fun for everyone.
I'll never forget the day Clifford and his friends learned about **FAIRNESS.**

Find stickers of flowers and bumblebees and put them on this page.

T-Bone was playing on a swing.
"Hurry, T-Bone!" Cleo said. "I'm next!"
Cleo could hardly wait for her turn.

Can you find a sticker of Cleo and place it next to the swing?

Use on Page 15

Use on Page 17

Use on Page 16

Use on Page 17

Use on Page 19

Use on Page 19

Use on Page 18

Use on Page 19

Use on Page 19

Use on Page 20

Use on Page 3

Use on Page 6

Use on Page 5

Use on Page 7

Use on Page 7

Use on Page 7

Use on Page 8

Use on Page 9

Use on Page 10

Use on Page 11

Use on Page 12

Use on Page 13

Use on Page 14

Use on Page 15

n Page 21

I CAN
SHARE
AND BE
FAIR

Use on Page 24

n Page 23

"Okay, Cleo," T-Bone said. "You go."
But before Cleo could get on
the swing, Mac rushed past her
and jumped on instead!
"Oh, boy!" he shouted. "This is fun!"

Find a sticker of Mac and put it on the swing.

13

Cleo was not happy.
"That wasn't fair," she said.
"It was my turn next."

Can you find a sticker of a squirrel and a bunny and put it in the park?

Clifford stopped the swing.
"Mac," he said, "we're supposed to take turns. That's the fair way to play."

Find stickers of Cleo and T-Bone and put them on this page.

"Oops!" said Mac. "I'm sorry, Cleo.
It's your turn."
"Thanks, Mac!" Cleo said.
And she happily took her place
on the swing.

Help Cleo take her turn by finding a sticker of her
and placing it on the swing.

16

For the rest of the day, Clifford and his friends all played **FAIRLY** and took turns—except when Clifford gave everyone a ride home. They all took a turn at once!

Find stickers of Clifford's friends and place them on his back.

17

Clifford and I know that **SHARING** makes playing with friends a lot more fun.
I remember when T-Bone and Cleo learned that lesson the hard way. . . .

Can you find a sticker of a large toy bone and place it in the yard?

Cleo and T-Bone both wanted to play
with the same toy bone.
"*Grr!* It's mine!" growled T-Bone,
tugging on one end.
"*Grr!* No, it's mine!" growled Cleo,
tugging on the other end.

Find stickers of other toys and put them on this page.

Suddenly, there was a loud *CRACK!*
Cleo and T-Bone had tugged too hard.
The toy bone was broken.

20

Put stickers of the broken bone next to Cleo and T-Bone.

Just then, Clifford arrived
and asked what had happened.
"I found this toy and it's mine!"
shouted Cleo.
"But I found it first!"
said T-Bone.

Can you find a sticker of Clifford to put on this page?

Clifford thought for a moment.
"Maybe instead of fighting over that toy,"
he said, "we can all share mine."
Cleo and T-Bone both thought that
was a great idea.

Can you find a sticker of Clifford's ball and put it on this page?

SHARING with each other made everyone happy.
Now the only tugging that happens
is during tug-of-war—and Clifford always wins!

*Find a sticker of Cleo and T-Bone
and put it on the end of the tug-of-war rope.*

23

As you can see, Clifford, Cleo, and T-Bone really do have a great time playing together.
And now you know how to share and be fair too!

Clifford THE BIG RED DOG®

_____
Name

knows how to Share and Be Fair

Find your "I Can Share and Be Fair" award sticker and put it on this page.